D1522874

FIESTA!

COLOMBIA

GROLIER

An Imprint of Scholastic Library Publishing
Danbury, Connecticut

Published for Grolier,
an imprint of Scholastic Library Publishing
Old Sherman Turnpike, Danbury, Connecticut 06816
by Times Editions,
an imprint of Times Media Pte Ltd

Copyright © 2004 Times Media Pte Ltd, Singapore
First Grolier Printing 2004

Set ISBN: 0-7172-5788-6
Volume ISBN: 0-7172-5791-6

Library of Congress Cataloging-in-Publication Data
Colombia.
p. cm.—(Fiesta!)
Summary: Discusses the festivals and holidays of Colombia and how the songs, food,
and traditions associated with these celebrations reflect the culture of the people.
1. Festivals—Colombia—Juvenile literature. 2. Colombia—Social life and customs—Juvenile literature.
[1. Festivals—Colombia. 2. Holidays—Colombia. 3. Colombia—Social life and customs.]
I. Grolier (Firm). II. Fiesta! (Danbury, Conn.)
GT4835.A2C65   2004
394.26861—dc21   2003044844

For this volume
Author: Tan Mae Lynn
Editor: Lynelle Seow
Designer: Geoslyn Lim
Production: Nor Sidah Haron
Crafts and Recipes produced by Stephen Russell

Printed in Malaysia

Adult supervision advised for all crafts and recipes,
particularly those involving sharp instruments and heat.

CONTENTS

COLOMBIA:

Colombia is the fourth largest country in South America. The country's name orginates from Christopher Columbus, who discovered the Americas.

▼ **Colombian coffee** is famous for its taste and quality. The country's soil and climate promote the growth of quality coffee beans, and there is a fresh supply of coffee beans all year round.

▼ **The Salt Cathedral of Zipaquira** is a church built from the walls of a salt mine. It can hold 10,000 people during Mass. An overwhelming majority of Colombians are Roman Catholic. The church plays an important role in the lives of most Colombians, and Catholic festivals and observations are widely celebrated in the country.

▶ **Emeralds** can be found in Colombia. The country is the world's biggest producer of emeralds. Colombians believe these gemstones possess special powers that can heal, make one smarter, reveal the truth, and block magic spells.

CARIBBEAN
SEA

Barranquilla

Valledupar

PANAMA

Cartagena

Mompox

VENEZUELA

Antioquia

PACIFIC
OCEAN

Cauca Valley

BOGOTÁ

Cali

Pasto

BRAZIL

ECUADOR

PERU

◀ **Santa Fé de Bogotá,** more commonly
known as Bogotá, is the capital of Colombia. Bogotá
is the largest city in the country and is the political
and industrial center of the nation.

RELIGIONS

Almost all Colombians are Roman Catholic. The Roman Catholic Church in Colombia is perhaps the most traditional Roman Catholic Church in South America. Many national holidays are influenced by Catholic celebrations.

THE PEOPLE OF COLOMBIA come from diverse backgrounds. Over half the population is *mestizo* (white-Indian descent), with the remaining half consisting of whites, *mulattoes* (black-white descent), *zambos* (black-Indian descent), blacks, and Indians. Yet despite its racial diversity, Colombian attitudes toward religion are fairly similar.

About 90 percent of Colombians are Roman Catholic. They are said to be the most devout followers of the faith compared with other South American Catholics. Before 1973 Catholicism was the official state religion of Colombia. A constitution change in 1973 meant that the church had less control over state issues like education and land. Even Catholic marriages now have to be recorded in the civil registry, and civil marriages are allowed.

Despite these changes, the Catholic Church remains strong in everyday life. The parish priest is a highly respected man. Catholic practices are important

The rosary is part of Catholic worship. The beads help keep count of a set of repeated prayers.

to Colombians; that is why church attendance is usually good. Religious days are taken seriously, and most of the country's national holidays and festivals are related to Catholic celebrations like Lent, Easter, and Christmas.

Other religious groups in Colombia exist, but are small in number. Protestants number about 200,000. There are even fewer Jewish people; they reside mostly in the larger cities of Colombia.

Catholicism has also influenced the native peoples. Only a few Indian tribes still practice their traditional beliefs. Most of them live in the remote and isolated parts of Colombia.

GREETINGS FROM **COLOMBIA!**

The official language of Colombia is Spanish. The influence of Spanish colonizers and early European immigrants on the country was so great that despite the country's racial diversity, almost every person speaks Spanish. Even Colombia's native population speaks Spanish too.

There are about 75 native languages, but only four percent of Colombians still speak them. As with most countries, there are regional accents that differentiate Colombians from different areas. Accents also differ between city dwellers and rural inhabitants. The way one uses the language is said to reflect his or her social class and educational background.

How do you say...

Hello
Hola!

Goodbye
Adiós!

Thank you
Gracias

Peace
Paz

Good morning
Buenos días

7

CHRISTMAS

Christmas is a Christian holiday that celebrates the birth of Jesus Christ on December 25. In Colombia celebrations end on January 6, the day of Epiphany. This day marks the arrival of the three wise men at the manger where Jesus was born.

Christmas celebrations in Colombia begin on December 7, the eve of the day of the Immaculate Conception, or the "Candle Light" day. This is when candles are lighted along street edges across the country to honor the Virgin Mary.

The following day, the day of the Immaculate Conception, is a national holiday and a day that Colombians attend Mass. Families place lighted candles on sidewalks. City streets and parks are also decorated with Christmas lights to add to the atmosphere.

Novena, marking the countdown to Christmas, begins on December 16.

Families put up their Christmas decorations and in their homes build the nativity scene that they will gather around to

The Nativity scene is called a pesebre *in Colombia.*

pray for the next nine days till Christmas. The cradle for baby Jesus stays empty until Christmas Eve. Only then will baby Jesus be put into it.

Western culture has brought the Christmas tree and Santa Claus to Colombia. Christmas trees are decorated with lights, ornaments, and cotton puffs. Traditionally the people believe that Jesus brings gifts on Epiphany. Although some people still believe this legend, today many others think that it is Santa Claus that brings the presents at Christmas.

In the Cauca River Valley children play a game called "Shouted Christmas Presents" on Christmas Eve. This is how the game is played. Two leaders assemble a team with an equal number of members. Each member on the team wears the same costume. The two teams meet, and the leaders must try to identify each other without speaking.

In Colombia Santa leaves presents at the foot of the beds of good children.

Happy Christmas! Happy Christmas!
Happy Christmas! Prosperous year and happiness!
Happy Christmas! Happy Christmas!
Happy Christmas! Prosperous year and happiness!

SONG: FELIZ NAVIDAD!

Fe – liz Na –vi dad!– – – – Fe-

liz Na –vi dad!– – – – Fe-

liz Na –vi dad! Pros–pe –ro año y

fe – li – ci –dad!– – – –

CALI FAIR

The Cali Fair is celebrated at the end of the year from December 25 to December 30. It is a festive occasion full of salsa parties, parades, bullfights, and a beauty pageant.

The city and people of Cali are proud to be known as the salsa capital of Colombia. That is because every year many salsa bands can be seen performing day and night on the streets.

The fair usually begins with a parade of cavalry along the main streets of the town center. During the rest of the day performances by local singers, international players, and salsa bands with their dancers delight the crowd with music. Visitors and locals get to enjoy all sorts of music: *cumbia reggae,* which is an Afro-Caribbean rhythm; traditional sounds; and contemporary tunes. An event called the Festival of Orchestras also takes place to provide more musical entertainment. Some of the salsa bands and dancers that perform are highly acclaimed musicians who have performed in New York City. Others are local players hoping to become famous one day.

Throughout the one week-long festival the atmosphere is carnival-like. Cali's streets are alive with people dancing, relaxing, feasting on local food, and even shopping. During the day a "Fair of the Children" lets the

Salsa is a Latin American music genre that originated in New York.

young ones participate in the celebration too.

A popular attraction at the Cali Fair is the *Fiesta Brava* — a bullfighting event. Every year at the Cañaveralejo Bull Ring large crowds gather to watch the best bulls and bullfighters from Europe and the Americas fight it out against each other.

Like most South American festivals, the Cali Fair is not without its own parade of floats and beauty queens. All can enjoy the beautifully decorated floats, some with lights, sound, and beauty queens on board. The parade ends with the crowning of the new Señorita Cali, a girl picked from all the beauties at the annual Cali Fair beauty pageant.

NATILLA

Natilla is a sweet custard somewhat like vanilla pudding. It is easy to make and delicious. Other ingredients such as raisins can be added to the recipe. Most people prefer to eat it plain.

YOU WILL NEED
1 quart milk
1½ cups cornstarch
1½ cups brown sugar
4 or 5 cinnamon sticks or ground cinnamon to taste
1 small coconut, shredded

1 Dissolve the cornstarch in the milk.

2 Add the brown sugar to the mixture.

3 Cook the mixture over low heat while stirring it all the time.

4 When the sugar is melted and the mixture begins to thicken, add the cinnamon and coconut.

5 When the natilla is very thick, pour into a large serving dish.

DAY OF THE BLACKS/ FESTIVAL OF THE WHITE ONES

These two festivals are celebrated by smearing shoe polish and throwing talcum powder on anyone out on the streets. It can be a messy affair, but everyone has a good time.

The Day of the Blacks (*Día de Negritos*) falls on January 5, followed by the Festival of the White Ones (*Fiesta de los Blanquitos*), which is on January 6.

The two festivals are celebrated in most cities, especially those located in the southern regions of Colombia, such as the city of Pasto.

The origins of the Day of the Blacks began in 1607 in the Antioquia region. The black slaves living there had created a stir because they were unhappy that they had to work all year round

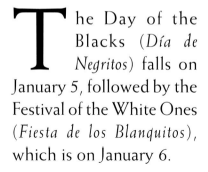

Flour and water are mixed together to form a sticky mixture that ladies pour over people walking below their balconies.

without any rest. They brought their petition to the King of Spain, and he granted them one free day a year — January 5. The slaves were so overjoyed at their new "freedom" that they went onto the streets in celebration. Such was their joy that they even used coal to paint the faces of people, even white people.

This face-painting tradition continues to be part of the celebrations today. The day begins with boys going out on the street with black shoe polish. They run after girls to smear black polish on their faces, but everyone who goes out in public is liable to get the black polish smeared on his or her face, hands, and body. In the afternoon there are parades in the streets. People are in elaborate masks, and musicians enliven the mood with their tunes. The main attraction of the day is the parade of floats featuring colorful moving figures. Participants dress in costumes that tell of Colombian folklore and culture. All the wealthy farmers of the town also make food donations in the main square.

The Festival of the White Ones, which occurs on the following day, is celebrated in the same way but in white. People get flour or talcum powder thrown at them. By the end of the day the streets are white with flour. Like the day before, there are parades with participants dressed in costumes and masks demonstrating the traditional skill of the craftsmen of Pasto. The history behind the Festival of the White Ones is not as widely known. Some say the spraying of talcum powder has its roots in an incident in the early 1900s when a man snatched a lady's powder puff and dusted his friends with it.

During the second day of the festivities the boys in the town are armed with white powder, which they toss on anyone they see.

CANDLEMAS

**Candlemas, or the Feast of the Virgin of La Candelaria,
is an annual event that brings people from all over the country
to the town of Cartagena to celebrate and pray for blessings.
It is celebrated on February 2.**

The Virgin of Candelaria is the patron saint of Cartagena and is believed to protect the residents of the city from plague and pirates. Her statue is kept in an old convent church, the Church of Santa Cruz, located on La Popa Hill, the highest hill in the city. In the evening hundreds of people climb the hill carrying lighted candles to pray. The Virgin's statue, decorated with flowers, leads the procession of the faithful up to the church. At the base of the hill dancing and singing can be heard, sometimes all through the night.

In the church itself hundreds of candles are blessed. There are candles of several colors, each color having a different purpose. The blessed candles are distributed to followers and are used differently; some candles give light during a storm, some drive away witches and evil spirits, and some protect the family and their animals from diseases. White candles are reserved for religious ceremonies such as in the Candlemas procession, during Easter, and on Christmas. Yellow candles are usually used for funerals.

*White candles represent joy. That is why
Easter and Christmas candles are white.*

Many believe that the light from the blessed candles is particularly important to women who want to have a baby or to find husbands. That is why in some Colombian cities Candlemas celebrations are for women only. In some other places the procession and celebration of Candlemas take to the fields, for it is believed that the number of candles blown out by the wind tells how good the year ahead will be.

Each type of candle symbolizes something different; votive candles mean a prayer going up to God.

THE USE OF CANDLES IN WORSHIP

The word "candle" comes from a word meaning to shine. The candle is believed to be a good symbol of God. The different parts of a candle each represent certain divine characteristics; for example, the wax represents Christ's clean and spotless body. The wick represents the soul of Jesus. The glowing flame symbolizes God as the light of the world. Special candles can be used in Catholic worship: The Advent candle counts the days until Christmas; the Baptismal candle symbolizes the passing from darkness into light; and the Easter candle symbolizes the light of the resurrection of Jesus Christ.

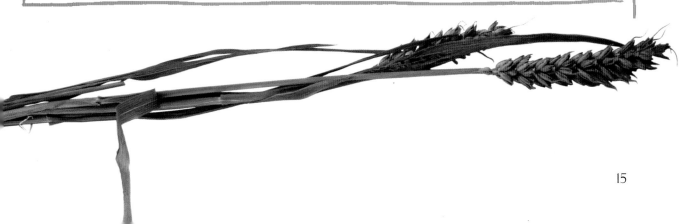

CARNAVAL

Carnaval, *or Carnival, is the biggest fiesta celebration of the year. It is celebrated a few days before the start of Lent in late February or early March. It is a vibrant event of parades and salsa parties with lots of costumes, masks, music, and dance.*

The Carnival has a long history that dates back many centuries to Europe. It was brought over to the Americas by the Spaniards and Portuguese.

The most famous Carnival parade is held in Barranquilla. Dance troupes can be seen parading through the streets rehearsing for the actual event. Even the Carnival Queen is chosen in October of the previous year so that she can be well prepared for the demands of the event. Another interesting person chosen early is King Momo. The person who plays this character must be well known for his joyous spirit and must have had participated in Carnivals since he was a child.

At the end of weeks of rehearsals a carnival proclamation is read out stating that everyone must enjoy himself or herself during the Carnival!

In Barranquilla the parade begins with floats, followed by the Carnival Queen dancing through the streets. Festive music is played by the best carnival band. During this week of carnival partying there is a dizzying selection of dance rhythms like the

merengue, cumbia, and salsa. Ritual dances, many of which are influenced by African traditions, can also be seen. Another dance, the coyongo, named for a bird that feeds on fish, has participants wearing bird costumes and masks with beaks. In this dance drama several of the birds attack a "fish" that must try to escape from them.

An orchestra festival is held on one of the carnival days. It is a competition of various Latin bands.

The carnival ends with the burial of "Joselito Carnaval," who is put to rest till the next Carnival.

AREPAS

Arepas are a type of bread. They can be eaten with almost anything.

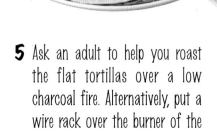

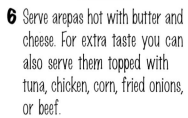

YOU WILL NEED

1 cup precooked white cornmeal
1 cup water
butter
1 teaspoon salt

1 Ask an adult to help you bring water to a boil.

2 Add the cornmeal, and stir thoroughly.

3 Add some butter and salt to taste.

4 Using your hands, form it into several flat tortillas (about 1/4" thick).

5 Ask an adult to help you roast the flat tortillas over a low charcoal fire. Alternatively, put a wire rack over the burner of the stove and roast.

6 Serve arepas hot with butter and cheese. For extra taste you can also serve them topped with tuna, chicken, corn, fried onions, or beef.

SEMANA SANTA

Semana Santa, or Holy Week, is the most important religious festival in Colombia. Celebrations during the week are both solemn and full of cheer. It is celebrated in either March or April. The date is decided by the Catholic Church each year.

Semana Santa is a time to celebrate the final days of Jesus Christ's life and the end of Lent. It begins as early as Thursday and continues through Good Friday until *Pascua*, or Easter. Good Friday is the most important event in Colombia other than Christmas. It is a joyous day celebrated with Mass in church, Eucharistic rites, and processions.

In Mompox people dress in turquoise robes and then lead others to the Immaculate Conception Church. There they throw stones and kick at the doors to gain entry. Once in the church, their robes are blessed during Mass. Church activities and celebrations can continue the following day as early as four in the morning.

On Palm Sunday the people celebrate by attending Mass in church. This is then followed by a procession to remember Jesus Christ's entry into Jerusalem.

Semana Santa is often characterized by religious processions all over the country. People dress in costumes and put on reenactments of Jesus Christ's final days. It is an emotional experience for the hundreds of faithful devotees following the processions.

Special robes are worn by the men leading the Semana Santa procession.

On Easter Sunday the mood changes from sorrow to joy. Mass is celebrated in church, and festivities are full of cheer to celebrate Jesus Christ's resurrection. Western influence has made the Easter egg a symbol of Easter in Colombia

EASTER

Easter celebrates the resurrection of Jesus Christ, who Christians believe died for the sins of all of mankind. He was crucified on a wooden cross on Good Friday. Three days after, on Easter Sunday, Jesus rose from the dead.

Most Christians observe Easter on the first Sunday after the full moon of Spring. This means Easter can fall on any Sunday between March 22 and April 25. The period leading up to Easter is known as Lent. Holy week is the final week of Lent.

EASTER EGGS

The egg is perhaps the oldest and most universal symbol of rebirth and new life. It aptly symbolizes the hope and joy of the resurrection of Jesus Christ.

The custom of offering Easter eggs, either chocolate or hard-boiled and colored, began with the pagan cultures of the Egyptians and Persians, who dyed eggs in spring colors and gave them to friends.

MAKE A CROSS NECKLACE

To Christians the symbol of the Cross is a reminder of the suffering of Jesus Christ. The Cross can be found in almost all churches. Some believers choose to wear the Cross around their necks so that they always feel thankful for the great sacrifice Jesus made by dying on the Cross.

YOU WILL NEED
Popsicle sticks
Drill
Aquarium rocks
Craft glue
Yarn
Scissors

1 Ask an adult to help you drill a small hole on one end of a Popsicle stick.

4 Apply glue to the front of the cross.

5 Place the cross face down into the aquarium rocks. Move it a little, and push down so the rocks will stick.

6 Put the cross down, and let it dry.

7 Cut a piece of yarn long enough to be a necklace.

8 Once the cross is dry, thread the yarn through the drill hole, and tie the two ends in a knot.

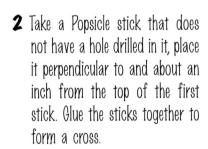

2 Take a Popsicle stick that does not have a hole drilled in it, place it perpendicular to and about an inch from the top of the first stick. Glue the sticks together to form a cross.

3 Write your name on the back of the cross.

THE WEEPING ONE

The Weeping One is a sad story of a woman named Maria who threw her children into the river because she was angry with her husband. Villagers say that her spirit has been calling out to her dead children ever since.

MANY YEARS AGO, in a small village there lived a beautiful girl named Maria. Because of her beauty Maria thought she was better than everyone.

As Maria got older, she became more beautiful, but her pride also grew. She refused to give the young men from her village a chance to get to know her because she thought they were not good enough for her.

"When I marry, I will marry the most handsome man in the world," Maria would often say to others.

One day a handsome young man rode into Maria's village. He seemed just what Maria had been looking for. He was the son of a wealthy ranch owner and a skilled horse rider. He could rope a wild horse, as well as play the guitar and sing. Maria planned to get his attention.

Maria decided that she needed to be coy; if she met him on the pathway and he tried to talk to her, she would look the other way; or when he serenaded her at her house, she wouldn't go to the window. She even turned down all his gifts.

Everything went as Maria had planned. The young *ranchero* fell for Maria's tricks. Soon they were married. They had two children and were a happy family. But it didn't last long. After a few years Maria's husband returned to the wild life on the plains. He disappeared from town for months at a time, returning only to visit his children. He appeared to have grown tired of Maria and even spoke of marrying another woman. Maria soon became jealous of her children because of all the attention they received from her husband.

One day while she was strolling along the river with the children, Maria's husband pulled up in a carriage. Maria was very surprised to see an elegant lady sitting next to her husband. They spoke a while with the children. Then, without looking at Maria, the pair rode off again.

Maria was filled with rage. Without thinking, she grabbed her two children and threw them into the river! As they disappeared downstream, Maria suddenly realized what she had done. She raced down the riverbank, stretching out her arms to save them, but it was too late.

The next morning Maria's body was found by the river. On that very night the villagers claimed they heard a woman crying by the river's edge. At first they thought it was the wind, but it was *La Llorona*, or the weeping woman, crying, "Where are my children?" From then on they would often see a woman walking up and down the riverbank crying for her children. She was dressed in a long white robe, the same clothes Maria was wearing.

All children know of her till this day. Parents warn their young ones not to go out at night because *La Llorona* will snatch them away forever.

CORPUS CHRISTI

Corpus Christi is a celebration of the Eucharist 60 days after Easter. It is an important national holiday with celebrations and activities held across the country in May or June each year.

Colombian girls wear white dresses on their First Communion.

Catholics celebrate Corpus Christi by going to Mass and participating in other religious activities. In the rural parts of Colombia observations of the day are more solemn.

In the Eucharistic procession the Host, or Holy Communion, is often carried on an elaborately decorated altar surrounded by priests and devotees.

This day is also special because the First Communion is often celebrated. Young children are dressed all in white when they receive their very first Communion. This is an important event for all Catholic families. Many parents spend a lot of money on their children's clothes for this day.

Corpus Christi is also a colorful festival. Groups of people get together to try to build the most beautiful alter. Using simple materials, they create scenes or objects from the Bible. They then line them proudly along the streets to showcase the works of art. Competition is fierce, but the results are spectacular.

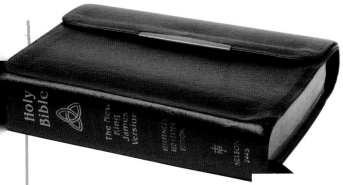

MAKE A BIBLE DECORATION

The Bible is the sacred book of Christianity. Some bibles are beautifully decorated with gold or precious jewels to reflect the importance of their content.

YOU WILL NEED

Black felt
Cardboard soap box
Glue
Gold or yellow ribbon for sides of soap box
Gold marker pen

1 Cut the black felt to cover the front side, one side, and the back of your soap box. Then use the glue to stick the felt onto the box.

2 Take your ribbon, and use your glue to stick it to the remaining edges of the soap box that is not covered with felt.

3 Use the gold marker pen to write the letters "BIBLE," and draw a cross on the one side of the box. If you prefer, you can use watercolor paint for the word "BIBLE."

4 Your bible is now ready to be used as a craft in festive decorations!

THE LEGEND OF EL DORADO

The Legend of El Dorado, or the "gilded man," is a centuries-old story about a native Indian king whose body was covered with powdered gold. It is believed that he still appears to his people.

TO THE SPANISH COLONIZERS looking for gold and treasures, the native Indians, or Muiscas, intrigued them. The natives were rich in gold and seemed to have obtained their wealth from a place outside their home towns. From some captured natives the Spaniards began to hear of a legendary king and leader by the name of El Dorado.

The legend begins with the spiritual ceremony of appointing El Dorado the new leader. As part of the rites, the king was to journey out to the great lagoon of Guatavita to make an offering to the gods. An elaborately decorated raft was made and loaded with all sorts of treasures from the village to be used as a sacrifice.

On the day of the ceremony the king was stripped to his skin. He was then anointed with sticky oil and completely covered with gold dust. As the raft pushed off shore, the smoke from burning torches and incense, resin, and other perfumes shrouded the area in darkness. The king was accompanied by four chiefs decked in crowns, bracelets, pendants, and ear rings – all of gold. They each carried their own offerings.

When the raft reached the center of the lagoon, a banner was raised as a sign calling for silence. The gilded man then threw out the piles of gold and treasure into the center of the lake. As he headed to shore, the villagers celebrated

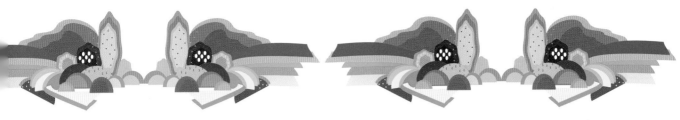

with song and dance. They were happy that a new ruler had been received and recognized as king. The gold offerings would also ensure that the villagers would be protected and blessed with wealth.

Since then it is believed El Dorado sometimes appears to his people by a lake in the mountains. He pushes a raft to the lake's center and throws gold into the water. Then he disappears into the waters of the lake. That is why the king and the promise of gold have fascinated humankind for centuries.

INDEPENDENCE DAY

Colombians fought long and hard against the Spanish colonizers to gain their independence. Finally, in August 1819 independence was declared.

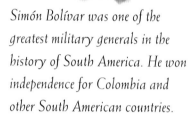

Colombia celebrates its Independence Day on July 20. The country's struggle for independence began in the 1790s after the French Revolution. Revolutions in 1796 and again in 1806 were unsuccessful attempts to form an independent government in Bogotá.

The city of Cartagena declared its independence in May of 1810. Bogotá followed one month later, but independence did not last long. Spain managed to regain the territory six years later in 1816. It was only in August 1819 that independence was finally declared after a brave man, Simón Bolívar, led the fight against the Spaniards and defeated them at the famous Battle of Boyacá. Colombia was previously known as Nueva Granada. It only took the name Colombia in 1863.

As Independence Day approaches, the Colombian flag can be seen displayed outside homes. Young students celebrate the day by giving

Simón Bolívar was one of the greatest military generals in the history of South America. He won independence for Colombia and other South American countries.

plays and performances related to the Colombian culture. Festivities include singing patriotic songs, dancing, and eating various Colombian foods.

Parades are a common sight on this national holiday. Some Colombians dress in colonial costumes and participate in the parades, singing patriotic songs. Festivities can carry on well into the night, with dancers performing and celebrating in the capital city.

HIMNO NACIONAL

Oh glo – ria in –mar– ces –ible! Oh

jú – bi–lo in –mor –tal! En

sur – cos de do–lo – res E – l

bi – en ger–mi –na – ya El–

bi – en ger – mi – na– ya

Oh gloria in–mar–ce – si – ble!

Oh júbi– lo in –mor –tal! En

sur – cos de do–lor – es El bi–

en ger – mi –na – yah

Oh unfading glory!
Oh immortal joy!
In furrows of pain
Good is already germinating.

FESTIVAL DE LA LEYENDA VALLENATA

This means the "Festival of the Vallenata Legend," a festival that celebrates the folk culture of the town of Valledupar. It is also one of the largest festivals in the world that celebrates accordion music.

The first accordion came to Colombia in the late 1800s.

This annual festival, celebrated over three days in April, began 35 years ago to help continue the traditions of Valledupar music and Colombian myths and customs. It is also a day for celebrating the music of Vallenata, which is characterized by the sounds of the accordion and a percussion instrument called the *guacharaca*. An annual competition is held for the best accordion player.

Vallenata music came from the northeastern part of Colombia. "Vallenatos" was a mean name used for the poor who lived along the river valley and who suffered from a terrible disease that left their skin dry and flaky. Musicians were typically the most notorious of the poor because of the noise they made. They too became identified with the undesirable "Vallenatos."

Now musicians from all over the country come to Valledupar hoping to be crowned *El Rey Vallenato* — The Vallenato King. All visitors are able to enjoy performances by many groups in various locations around town.

Besides music, the town celebrates its culture with traditional dances, performances of local myths and legends, and a showcase of regional crafts.

WORDS TO KNOW

Cavalry: A group of soldiers or troops mounted on horses.

Eucharist: The consecrated bread and wine used and consumed in the Catholic ceremony commemorating Christ's last supper.

Floats: A platform built onto a truck that is elaborately decorated with various things or people; usually used in parades.

Folklore: Traditional beliefs, stories, or customs passed down through word of mouth over generations.

Gilded: To be covered with a thin layer of gold.

Legend: A traditional story from the past, usually passed down through generations from oral traditions; they may or may not be true.

Mass: A religious service of the Catholic Church.

Myth: A story or widely held belief that is not true.

Nativity scene: The representation of the birth of Jesus in the manger at Bethlehem.

Parade: A public procession with a display of things or people.

Patron saint: A saint who protects and guides a person, people, state, or nation.

Patriotism: The feeling of strong support shown by people toward their country.

Percussion: A musical instrument similar to the drums that is played by being struck or shaken.

Reenactment: A depiction of an event.

Resurrection: The rising of Jesus Christ into Heaven.

Sacred: That which is considered holy.

Salsa: Latin American music and dance with jazz and rock elements.

ACKNOWLEDGMENTS

WITH THANKS TO:
Anna Seah, Benjamin Yap, Chng Eu-Lee, Eunice Sin, Yap Eng Beng.

PHOTOGRAPHS BY:
Haga Library Japan (cover), Sam Yeo (p. 16 top left, p. 18 top right), and Yu Hui Ying (all other images).

ILLUSTRATIONS BY:
Cake (p. 1, pp. 4-5, p. 29) and Enrico Sallustio (p. 23, p. 27).

SET CONTENTS

32